# Travelers

Also by David Michael Belczyk

Somniloquy: Poems
Unexpected Guest: Poems
Called Perpetual: Poems
Forms and Vessels: Poems
The First Act of Creation
The Final Act of Creation
Nine Lessons
City of Bridges
Elynia

# Travelers

**DAVID MICHAEL BELCZYK**

**POEMS**

CIRCLING RIVERS
RICHMOND, VIRGINIA

Copyright © 2023 by David Michael Belczyk

All rights reserved. No part of this book may be reproduced in any form, including electronic, without permission in writing from the author.

## CIRCLING RIVERS
PO Box 8291
Richmond, VA 23226
CirclingRivers.com

Visit CirclingRivers.com to subscribe to news of our authors and books, including book giveaways. We never share or sell our list.

ISBN: 978-1-939530-34-9 (paper)
ISBN: 978-1-939530-35-6 (hardcover)

Library of Congress Control Number: 2023934530

Cover photo by David Michael Belczyk
Author photo by Joe Indovina

to my children

# Contents

Dedication | 5

## Cities | 11
Rome | 13
Paris | 14
Hong Kong | 16
Atlanta | 17
Oklahoma City | 18
Charleston | 19
Dublin | 20
Bayeux | 22
Barcelona | 23
Granada | 24
Seville | 26
Toledo | 30

## Habitations | 33
Oakland | 35
Sewickley | 38
Harmony | 40
Chapel Hill | 41
Hanceville | 42
Columbus | 43
Shenandoah | 44
Indianapolis | 45
Ligonier | 46
Ambridge | 47

## Departures | 49
Peoria | 51
Bridgewater | 52
Asheville | 54
San Francisco | 55
Rochester | 56
Dallas | 57
Cleveland | 58
Chicago | 59
Confluence | 61
Pittsburgh | 63

## Deserts | 65
Sedona | 67
Supai | 68
Monument Valley | 70
Phoenix | 71
Indiana Dunes | 72
Las Vegas | 73
Escalante | 75

## Stone | 77
Stratford | 79
London | 80
Tarentum | 82
Philadelphia | 83
York | 85
Corbett | 86
Bedford | 87

Milwaukee | 88
New Orleans | 89
Bath | 90

## Water | 91
Rehoboth | 93
Mackinac | 94
Clearwater | 95
Michigan | 96
South Padre | 97
Newport | 98
Erie | 99
Nantucket | 101
Bodensee | 103
Laguna | 104
Berkeley Springs | 105
Port Washington | 106
Niagara | 107

## Arrivals | 109
Gratoit | 111
Nice | 112
Edgeworth | 113
Myrtle Beach | 114
Moraine | 116
Emlenton | 118
Gettysburg | 119
Detroit | 121
San Juan | 122

# Travelers

# Cities

# Rome

I want from you what I already have
To travel the burden of love
To be left alone

A death of peace
In the far away
With untouchable hopes

I would see you
In other eyes
I would surrender again

And you would lead me
Your unchanging path

Within your myriad temples
New kisses on your many faces
Enclosed and enclosing life

And not memory
Surprised at the night when I wish
It has been only you all along.

## Paris

Light falls upon you
In streets
Your face like a window I used to
Look from
I gave you
Everything I could not say
And you made of my want
Steps to an unspoken heaven

Ancient plots and closures
And uprisings
Wind the broken way
A bouquet of unbalanced
Promises
Unfolded by time
A countenance between the pages
I carry
Not of you
But everything that became you

Nothing else
Straight as the view across roofs
To futures
Shrined on the pasts
Of hilltops
On a body of sunsets
That lies down to promises

I am bound to you by
The honeyed afternoon
From the basements
Where we eat
To the hollows of radiant heights
Streets tie fetters
The fathoms of words.

## Hong Kong

You gave me into many arms
Flowers upon
Ancient gnarled roots
That cling to stone walls
To overtop them
That wend through multitudes
And quiet cobbled closes
You gave me into
The old and the new

An island wanting
To know its ocean
A pilgrim
Looking for an island
In clouds of incense
Portals in temples
Enclosed in gardens
And creeds
The things you said you were not

Up the steps
To a little table
At the intersection
Of a compass rose
Am I in my world
Or yours
Or will you find me
In an older one.

## Atlanta

I longed for you
When you surrounded me
And I could not have you
For your nearness

And temptation of perfect mystery
When my emptiness sang
With the flight of the wide world
You showed me your ache

And at your mercy
I let you go in mercy
Too different
And we too much the same

I look for you
A long way from our beginning
Changed but the same enough
To live for once a lifetime

To see not you
But what we share
Made of your image and my weakness
Your life in the grip of flight

Replaces mistaken youth
Adorned in hard-won wishes pure
You shall not wear.

## Oklahoma City

You alight
An altar of the ancient world
Unwinding over measureless prairies
Secret for their distances
Cut with roads
That lead to ruined capitals
And rivers drinking in the freckled sun
Winding the curves of winged serpents

A crown extends its branches
Over our young deaths
That bring me to your age
Late in the silent city
I remember sacrifices
Of ancient altars where I once stood
To waste what youth remains wrapped in your arms
A bed of maps from impossible places

The altar was destroyed and built again
Broken faces look on its stone
Innocent children and holy doors
An image of assembled fragments
Light will cross without breaking
And that is where I find you
On a ladder painting the ancient transom
Wood gnarled with age and fire and destruction
But wearing a golden crown

From your height you say
Walk through.

# Charleston

There is more dawn in you than day
Down unwalked alleys and snow omens
Whispers wash you from shore rushes
Once only lapping silence

Uncurl yourself in cloisters of driftwood
As long as the wandering lines
That circle the globe

I follow rising
The tide upon brambles
Tangles of petals upon a spine
Of brick and scars and words

I tread up steeples
To the center of your sonorous heart
A halo of storms and galleons
Turning seasons that make maps false

Silvery cobbles ring
Lengthening shadows
Where the face of night gathers

You brought me here
To tell me
There is no difference
Between night and day.

## Dublin

Cast me beneath your deepest questions
The flow of years slenders me
As labored breath
Formed in the architecture of millennia
Curved in the sacred past
The hope
And the steps of coming day

The lights kept on
Pull the darkness from us
In the flow of a long story

In the morning
We will be locked out
Of this transcendent moment
When motion makes a perfect face
That erodes as it is made
Everything

That opens
Is down there beneath the current
Where you place it inaccessible
I will cast it down

In one moment that is all time
In one discovery that lasts forever
One reckoning of all irretrievable gifts
Inseparable from me

A hand upon your chest
To feel the rise and fall of
Our struggle to live

A raised hand atop a revetment
Above the river's tide of city light
Holding the tiny thing I have carried so long
A key
Like a bird and like a bell

Enveloped in the clear and onward
I fill up the vacant night
With sound and falling
Shattering surfaces
All the things I meant to do
Dispersing light to inscrutable patterns

Making reflections
Of our past within and our future without
We will break the locks.

# Bayeux

In the morning
Soaring spires glide
Cool and pointed shadows
Empty streets are for us to fill
Creation unfolds at the end of our sight
Each way there is a way
To overcast shores at high tide

In the afternoon
The clouds divide
Incense dispersed
The streets are rising
To a jubilee of color and motion
That we missed
The places I remember are closed

There is only the long way
The long walk on sinking sand
With the tide far out
Under abundant sun
You reflect in pools left behind

I fear I will never see you again
I must come all the way
Across my life
To this place I remember

Never are the two the same
But the time the skies are parting.

# Barcelona

The first time
You showed me the vision of distances
The enduring self that climbs
Your abundant heights
Your summit that ever rises

Above your creation
Gazing over ages to the sea
A first conception
Of majesty
Upon your wings

I returned to you
Full of other selves
That came to me because of what you showed
So you took me to your depths
A cornerstone and a tomb in the earth
That cannot be seen from the clouds

And here the fulfillment
Of what I saw first
Your sacred fruit stretching
Unfinished.

# Granada

### I

There lay oceans between me
And the myth of you
And I thought
If I crossed them
Your body would be there

I came to drink your death
Among the nighttime maze of streets
And caverns of cities
Run my fingers over fragrant hilltop groves
And the pits of wells
The bottoms of glasses

The tombs are empty
The last home
Shared like bread

In a fortress besieged by millennia
And changing crowns
I have come to the door of flight
Never to be opened

I have come to the centennial keep
To a wedding inside the church
The bride's veil
Billows over uncrossable battlements
Out of respect
I do not enter

## II

In these conquered temples
Room after room adorned
With the search for your beauty
I have been here as an infant
So I dream of them all my life
And do not know where they are

I heard of you like faith
But long to touch
To hear in city corridors your tongue of flame
Sun blush upon you
So I am face to face

With the emptiness of your tomb
The surprise of you
The life left behind
And startled I
Inhale mornings

Ascend your winding streets
Cobbles and stairs
Above lamps and balconies
Above spires

To gaze on other dreams
That wed me to all
I could not know
One drink enclosed in stone
Beneath the veil of mountains.

# Seville

### I

An alcove in a garden wall surrounding
Aisles of palms through iron bars
Roses and fountains extend sightlines

Passing through the narrows
Reaching for expanses
Light dapples my clothes my skin
A breeze carries the perfume of blossoms

I take mouthfuls
Like it is your breath
Or my last breath

Elsewhere the walls are already crumbling
I may walk over them
But I rest here

### II

The day travels beyond sight
Beyond the curve of light
Borne aloft on the shoulders of kingdoms
Unmoving toward the further distance

The city
Continues unfolding and remaking
You are within the vessel
You are beyond the precipice

And I wonder how long
Will I see the skyline
How long before you knew what you would find


## III

I am to face the ageless
To struggle with my own death
In its powerful and beautiful body

It is how I live
It is all I know
How to do

And you will want to watch
And love and detest
All the wishes I drag with me
And all that watches

There is a little place
A sacred place for me
Hallowed by the ones that went before

There is one person there
Before I come
Before your eyes
It is also you

## IV

Illuminated in night
Above terracotta roofs and antennas and geraniums
You watch
Changes of faith and love
Seasons of gardens and fruit

Uplooking buildings
Remade upon the same ancient bones
Light-reflecting streets in silence
Crowds moving

Your spires and heights
Mark the graves of builders
Life consuming vacancy
Life consuming also life

I strain to hear the brooks and calls
From your immemorial
At last a moment of awe
Of revelry and promise and freedom
To a pilgrim

But for the ringing you have left in my ears
I cannot hear the midnight silence
I look to you to mark the flow of time

And you have seen me
Come into your streets from nowhere
And take your image in the night
Above gardens and caskets and killers
And the awfulness of not remembering

Illuminated doves
Soaring through endless space
Look like falling stars.

# Toledo

### I

Fresh and soft with sleep
And ancient bone impregnable
In you meet the different ways
I would go
Awakening those who leave all else behind

Surrounding walls sleep martyrs
Thrown down and plundered
Shelves hold the fires of conquerors
Murder prowling orange-scented arcades
Where today lies only peace

A cloister simple and placid
Effusive with function
Ornate with directness
Clay-tiled walks enclose a garden about the well

When the fierceness of your secret beauty
Means all wells must be sacred


### II

Beneath streets are buried streets
Buried pools beneath baptisms
Buried persecutions
Lost names filled
With rain that comes through remnants

A past that does not speak unknown
But comes to me in friends
I must listen
So you speak to me unknowns
In the fleeting peace

You speak in your own destruction
In tombs having all the eloquence of martyrs
And their many throats


### III

A puzzle of halls among ancient brick homes
Adjacent walls made and remade
Rooms that marry and divorce
Empires and lifetimes

Unsquared doors wrench open
Diverse arches blind with bricks
A decaying apse in modern wood
And unmatching stone

Together making your whole
In rooms made one
A sudden temple that has been their many sacred places

How did it come into this home
How did it come to be your room

## IV

Leaving with you an eternal city's blindness
Each vista and alley seems perfect
I even wish for my own tumult again

Because it belongs to you
And it may not be mine
It is because we are leaving
And me my treasured losses
That they mean anything

That you speak
In fragrant night and nectar
That closes placid eyes
And makes us deaths and pieces

Nothing makes sense unless it can be lost
No time unless it is ending
No place unless you are leaving.

# Habitations

# Oakland

### I

All the unbounded
Expanse that you are
Is within me

The knit of my flesh
Believes your life
And I know your death
And no one
Knows your name

Does your life or your death
Move in me
Bear fruit that I bear
Even what I know cannot
Convince my flesh

I go on making
All your futures
Protecting a tiny vessel
Of the infinite
That closes and opens

How do I know
What flesh does not
It understands the boundaries of the self
I have never seen
But I know your truth

**II**

Even as you died no one knew
Even in my mind you lived
Though you stopped within
How many heard your secret

One by one
Longed and learned
There was still a place in the world
Waiting

Until I told all
And there was
No one left


**III**

From my youth
Small boxes
Have fascinated me
To keep them
Open them

Dream of secrets
They might hold
I felt I had
Something sacred
To put in them

I did not know what it was
What I was
I did not know
It was you.

# Sewickley

## I

I took all of you
Your hopes became
One surrender
And poured out the life of the world
And everything I ever knew
And all that you left
And all that you bear
Cast itself in one fluid arc
Unerring and unchanging
And it was my name
Carrying change and the same childhood

## II

A lucid morning for a lifetime
A last conversation for all you taught me
For me to think of until I am there
In the bed
And it was just like it had always been
No one was coming
You woke to talk of nothing
An afternoon
With all the time we needed
I said I love you to the shudders of your breath
And when you looked
It was the last time I saw the color of your eyes

## III

You took all of me
Whatever I should have been or thought I was
In one unerring and unchanging direction following
Your precocious steps
Heavenward with the uncomprehending
Purity of your songs
The reason for histories and homes
I will die again
As life makes itself anew
For this afternoon of paradise
When the sun does not set
Over you
Becoming all things not meant for me.

## Harmony

In an empty bedroom
You could not stay
Listening

A sister's laughter
Mingled with tears
A young but wrinkled face
Swirling with memories

Some unimportant joke shared
Uncounted years ago

Lives surface
As we wake
Voices and breath and sound
Over an empty bed

Meant for you
And maybe

When I stretch out
After
And follow this laughter
Stretching to you

We will fill houses like lungs
With inconsequential beauty
Sit by me
Say all that remains unsaid.

# Chapel Hill

I love you in all the ways that I am fragments
Everything in me that is lost
Abandons itself to you
I crave you in my night of weakness

Find you in my own hurt self answering

I love you in all the ways that I am fragments
I hurt because I am bound in love to you
I accept it so you see why I am broken
You find what I wanted

To show you all along.

## Hanceville

You are the first of the morning
Even before the sun
When I face myself

You are a house made of the sun's rays
Golden walls do not enclose
Your shelter I cannot leave

I place my hands upon reflections
To know they are real
My looking back is the only end

Plaited with gray sky enlivening
Everything I could not have known of you
Before I entered.

# Columbus

Low plains
Bathe in light and bird calls
Whirling from the rush
The breeze pushes me
With you like wings

The time is tired as you are wakeful
It has been preparing
It is always the moment I am about to change

We descend from mountains
To seek the solace of vastness
In knots of scrub
And private clutches of trees

To mark the horizon
We will find ourselves on this fertile soil
Cut the rushes and turn the fields
Raise a city toward the sky
With unimaginable shapes

From its heights
My eyes like birds
Search for you hidden among new stems.

## Shenandoah

You speak in centuries
In lies I tell myself
To be my soft and rolling beauty

I wish for ecstatic heights
That slow and steady speech has destroyed
Brought mountains low

With incomprehensible time
And left this verdant pasture
For me to find

The lie I tell is not a lie
You will live forever
Bare rock become this febrile emerald

The lie I tell is that I lie
To not believe the truth
Of transfiguration

I move hungry eyes
My hands over downy heights and valleys
Is this what I wanted.

## Indianapolis

I washed my innocence in your fountain
And ran like a child
Through the places left of yourself

You see everything
Under the midwest sun
You could be shadowless

Drape yourself upon unknown spaces
Across my shoulders
Lighter than cities

From one shoulder to the next
Poured-out sunsets draw longer selves
Drenched in your overspilling twilight

Clothed in light cities rise
From the midnight prairie

And the water came down
Over our heavy clothes

Clear as your hands upon my face
Brushing aside our lost ways
Heavy as midnight filling my pockets
We closed our eyes to uplift our faces.

## Ligonier

In a forest of living gates
I climb surefooted through solitude and discovery
Sleeping in serene shade
Rocky ways lie open

Felled trees
Make a place in the wild
A table to eat
A roof for the weather

The walls do not have within them
The new years the trees stood
Wounded make crutches of the timber
I enter the broad mouths of their decay.

# Ambridge

It is hard to leave
And impossible
To return
I go in your certain elsewhere
And familiar obscured
Keep when I flee
Someplace unknown
To live over again
How we found each other

It is impossible to leave
A birthplace
And to keep
Who we were
And who we have not become
My future in your longer memory
Little houses we no longer own
However far I go
Upon our old streets.

# Departures

# Peoria

Farther places beyond place
Days beyond night
Where does hard earth bloom
Unburdened joy

Searching streets a stranger
Turning fields I do not own
Around the corner
Uncloseable vistas

Where I abandon what I long to find

Barefoot upon the shorn harvest
In my hands the distance
To give what I am given
It is sufficient.

## Bridgewater

You light the streets
Every lamp every flame
Gathered crowds
Every table every body
The mysteries of houses and their pasts
Nature and strangers
Watching from porches and over hilltops
What I do not see around corners

Bricks riverbanks and gutters
Boughs of spent petals
Fragrant in the city's summer crush
Lives within walls
The names of avenues
The order of the city in empty fields
Music from windows
Weddings in churches
Children expected
Unmarked graves beneath sidewalks

I am surprised
By the outlines that make your body
So that I do not know what I want
When I look at you
Carried across these vacant midnights
Your boundless image surrendered in circling touch
Endless hunger
Lucid perfection once in life's labor
Aching possession that will not be understood

In the moment you show me
Yourself I would do anything
I cannot see you through the way that I want you
You are all of my cities and none of my lives
What would I do
If I could touch could have
Could carry you into all streets
Into all nature before
Aloft upon whatever precious artifact I could afford
Would you stay so ageless.

## Asheville

Your silence grew in me
Filling me until it could be filled
Approaching from the humid shore
Rose crystal heights
From heights the unsure
Purple distance lying down
That takes your breath

From a mountain bed
Sun stains streets jagged with age
Your breath steals
From my mouth
More
More vision than truth
More ancient than this morning

And the silence
Where I like to wait and die
For you to breathe again
To return from the clarity of height
To the ripeness of your shores
Where my throat will burn.

## San Francisco

Does a ghost have flesh as I do

Fire spread across the land
And scarred the vineyards
Sweet fruit in the ash
When rains came
Wildflowers filled the scars
Every color hidden
In fire's light

I held your body close
Like the sobs of a final question
In which we were married
I remember everything you said
Everything hid
The scent of your tears
Sweetness of future meadows

Lay the married upon my ashes
Your petals against my parched earth
Hold your body to me
Fertile garden
To bury the flame
The wine sinking into scars
Fire in the taste

Does a ghost have flesh
As I do.

# Rochester

Before shuttered clapboard houses
A yellow sign reads
Deaf child area
No one slows for old and rusting signs
You are grown
You are gone
You have taken your deafness with you.

# Dallas

You open the plains
Wide enough to disappear
To stand the tall beside the humble
And go away from me
And the hurt we lie beside

I return to the place I found you
I might have even had you not
Come back

I am free when I imagine you gone
I must love you
If I know you

In other hands
Thousands of hands
Of night and forevers
I try to forget we go to them

But we return to where we came from
To make of pain a truth.

# Cleveland

On a bluff above the lake
Sky rolled over
The brow of ancestors' skulls
Darkening
Into unseeable distance

Climbing skyward
The moment I let go of you
Has within it both
The height and the fall

It is over quickly
And I want that day and tomorrow
And the far tumbling shore
And I want nothing but
That broken moment

The moment before is not enough
And nothing else could be as much

We watched a little kite with a snapped string
Crash down beyond a fence
Among beguiling houses
But we climbed
And could not find it there.

# Chicago

Dark waters surround an expanding light
I embrace you
We lie on waves of skylines
Receding

Renewing
The places we touched crumble

I recover myself
In memories
Washed blindly toward
The end of all roads

I cover you with memories
Speak to you with inherited pasts

So vast I forget
My own rooms among your myriad
Lines building and breaking

Moving in you
I owned a death
And carried it with pride
It made me strong
My arms closing like harbor walls
With unlit potential

Now I come to your monuments begging
And death carries me fearfully

Newness floods old places with
Unpossessable beauty
That does not know what we did

That I cannot have
Because we belong to each other.

# Confluence

Two rivers make a third
Or one is swallowed
You let me touch
The place where they join

Show me your secrets
That do not belong to me
No matter what I want
You are the answer

This is faith
This is dependence
Seeing all of you
I do not recognize who you are

But you know me
You give to me
Until I am a thief

You give me what I ask
And what I need
This is famine
This is fullness

And you want what you want
Everything I have owed
In love and justice
You are the victim
I am the victim

Careful of what I give
Unconcerned with all I took

This is trust
This is fear

Knowing who I am
Does not tell you where I am going
Only what I deserve
You could say the same

We could speak
Though I do not know what I am saying
As we do not know our secret ache
That touches one another.

# Pittsburgh

Time takes all
To its immeasurable self
Unpossessed
And unpossessing

My only possession
This frail self that holds all fleeting
Itself fleeting
Into the arms of memory

Dragging me
To what I will become immeasurably
Is it time
Is it time.

# Deserts

# Sedona

Untame and untouched
Wilderness that is not wild
Until I am within

The peace of your parched heat
Your vastness
Red and vacant tables
Return to me again and again
When I am sated

You came to me in the desert
To give me everything
You promised

Draped me in your radiant dawn
Spilled me in plumes of light over your shoulders
And I refused

Not knowing when I saw you I changed you
Even had you known me not

Now I am stretched upon empty tables
And you visit joyfully
Wave upon wave of your fertileness
The ocean that once covered these dry sands

I drew a shell from the ocean
And painted on it were desert mesas.

# Supai

### I

In a dry canyon
Water once flowed

Sunlight spills from the rim
To raw earth
Opened red

Splitting the parched rock
A tree reaches up
Dry tongues to outgrowing leaves

The color of your eyes I left
In inexhaustible brightness
Roots beneath my thirst

### II

Water spills prolific
From the rim in sacred veils
To carry away the rock
In its lucent mouth

I find beneath
The place from which I came
Rising stripped and crystalline
The pleasure and the pain of distances

I swim until shadows cover
The narrow canyon
And water turns cold


**III**


Rock carried in the water
Colors the canyon floor white
Making turquoise pools from sunlight

I am pulled over the rim
The color of every sky
Plunging into death and heaven

The judgment of sleep
For the long crossing.

# Monument Valley

The cup of sky is full
Of the time it takes
To carry away deserts

When mountains erode
Tongues of fire stand
As rock to fill the hollows of horizons
In the hollows of breath that wears away

How I wanted
The way I loved you
I did not know the time I had
Until there was no time to flee to you

This summit of our lonely self
This forever
This transfiguration
A canyon that could not enclose your sky

You form this future desert
With the image of our past
I do not kiss
My breath glows upon embodying embers

Canyons of sky
Where earth takes the place of air
And creative power
Still in silent majesty

A tongue annulled
Love given up.

# Phoenix

Our lives do not know
How to touch
Night collides them
In widening spaces
More distant than you appear
So silent
I hear the blood flow in my ears
So parched
Spilled red with dust
The glow of coastlines
Are drawn together
And cover in heat
What should have been
Serene and different

Stripped to my unknowing
You touched me
Against the place I could not dream
I would find myself
The dawn over the vastness
Vulnerable but unafraid
How to say
How to hear
That we should cherish more
This impossible
Our lives did not know
Finding makes the desert boundless
The moment flies outward
Parched lips search for sweetness.

## Indiana Dunes

We walk the jagged landscape
The cold made
Of the waves
Peaks upon our tongues
The sharp ice we ate
Trespassers upon the night
Upon unfathomed depth
You break the crystal thinness
Between us
The chrysalis of silence
The heat of your words
Dispels all fear we enter
The wilderness
Made for us

Upon heights the distance breaks
In sky blue
And clouds of foam
A circle of thorny scrub
We find a little hollow in bloom
The sun slicks your skin
Pricked all over with bites
More radiant
Than golden sands that stick to us
Embracing unknown intervals
With shielded eyes
The unattainable coast cools
Reflected in your sight
Circle peaks and valleys below.

## Las Vegas

Your crystal depths uncovered
Show the thirst that made canyons
And dried the desert
A gift from a faraway past
That I take home

I haven't enough tears
To make up the difference
Between unbridled time
And the emptiness it made
Then filled

I haven't enough
To cry out the heights
Between the fullness we were
And the clarity
Of thirst

I haven't the time
Rivers of patience
And the chalky distance
Between high water
And tears

A ribbon stranded above
Profound sapphire
Below the sky we reflect
A veil
Pulled tight over my face

I breathe slowly the heat
That starts and stops
The river's weeping

Unsleeping I
Move over forms of the lost
Gifts of the unattainable
That drink deeply
The unintelligible
That point skyward

High I see shapes beneath
Flood waters too deep to drink
Their design of unpatterned evenings
The day lets go of me
There is no longer anything
I am supposed to do.

# Escalante

Across the length of nothingness
I unravel
The surge of life
That makes a place for us to kneel
To climb
Where we would have been
Breathless

Our path
A torrent of dry tongues
From a world before the flood
Made of that for which I thirst
The parted bones of paradise
Upon the high mesa
Where we break the forms
That gave us life

Nothing remains
Of the pouring water that opened
The fractured rock
And carried it away
Just drops of my own sweat
Upon the burning sand
You reach to me
A tendril of swirling incense

Crawling up a mystic
Web of arches
Acrobatic eddies
The impossible places you reach
Are so narrow I cannot breathe

Like my way to you is carving them
Instead of the lonely verdure
Before the desert

In fractals of the self
I pass through the fabric
Of what we see
Hand in hand

On higher mountains
Streams are still flowing
Cascading in ribbons to a glorious
Emerald eye
And there unshamed I crash
Into the frigid waters
And salt and sand
Stream out from my long hair.

# Stone

## Stratford

We come to a precipice
But a little devouring
Step
And across hides all we cannot touch

I come again to be fooled by dust
To be sealed under heavy stone
And leave nothing

The old hunger of the unseeing
Eats names into stones outside
Epitaphs wearing away
We came as close as we could

To see your uncovered depth
A stone font wailing with life cries
That are not consumed

That blanket the walls
And flee the town the horizon
The decaying stone
And this font I touch

On my side of the precipice.

# London

You encircle me a promise
Carried for a lifetime
Why do I come back to you
Where else would I go

Show me a dare I call beauty
Cut my tangled names
Show me a reckless selfish child I was
And how I wish

Show me city gardens
Uncovering lines
Perfect in stone
Where you know what I want
Am I so simple
To come back

To live in your need
As you
And I are the grave of my jealousy

Artifacts wash against your shores
Your tides
Replace who I was
In place of my eyes

You become my undone
Severed strands
You become an inescapable you

I come to the heart
Where the city turns to flesh
Alone a past
And a hope that do not kiss.

# Tarentum

A stone formed
Heavy with rest
Eons before

Our first word was spoken
Before we strode
Out of paradise

It lay beneath
Rulers and temples and idols
Autonomy and sufficiency

A little girl
On a sunny idle afternoon
When no one in particular watched

Lifted it
And split its sediment in two
Dark made light as the beginning
The hidden revealed.

## Philadelphia

You wait for me
At the end of the world
In your bed of tedious stone
In unenclosable dreams
That shape cities
And a body made from these things
Breaks with pleasure and pain

A cleft in the rock
I might hold
I might carry all my pasts with
Friends and failures
And enter
And find within
Your body
And what remains

A river I might cross
Into misunderstood dreams
And find out who you were
When I was so close
And shaping you
Is what shaped me

Through stone gardens
Sculptures and harbor markets
Towers of hope and prisons and saving
And not touching
All made of the same things
And choices in the old streets

Where how many before me
Even you
Went one way or the other

Into skylines waiting
That I leave behind
The horizon reaching toward you
Across my crumbling continent
To your bed
Unwritten
And unwritable.

# York

Beneath arches
We sip cold mornings
And lie in mists
You strip away like sheets
The colors of our mouths
The chill of our bones
And nights you spoke
In places that cannot be found

There is so much
I wish to tell you
That I could speak
In your future
That I could sleep
In your past
In sacred places that belong to others
I build my temples

The same
And unrecognizable river
That curved in the field
Before the fleshlike curve of stone
Enclosed and perfected
The hope of open spaces
I dally with you by the river
In the morning
The timeworn streets
Less ancient than where we are going.

# Corbett

I lie where you lay
A cavern so full of the shelter
You made with warmth and sleeping
A delicate script upon the rock
That speaks of one
Who found it first
Could you know
We would find this place
In your message

To have young life in the cave of my hands
Again
The flesh around which the rock
Was shaped for us to come
I take out the stuff of my name
And mark it in space
Against the infinite
Out of this I am made
The shelter hewn.

# Bedford

The blazing morning
Awakens my thirst
Tempts me to drink

I go to the mist and shadows
Of enclosing forest
A cold mouth spilling over
Transparent darkness
Lush with growth

Sweet with life and decay
Breathless power pours from deep earth
And I go under
Where sleep poisons the water
Your tireless flow carries it away

Further until the paths are meaningless
Dizzy with height
Folded in laurel
Bathed in solitude

There is your spring
And the secrets looking back
Beneath its luster.

## Milwaukee

Standing in the street we did not see
The quarry's depth
A ridge of grass
A copse of trees
Then desolation chilling to the bone
And you stood radiant upon the precipice
Ringed by sunken light

The fear that you would fall
Was looking up from the depth
A shape of stars and blackness
You fill all the space between the taken
And what remains

But looking at you fearless
Is like the falling
So I am the edge
And you the gulf
To show me something beyond this pit

The danger and its light
The seen and the unseen
You take me from the city to these secret places
To stand at the lip of graves.

# New Orleans

When I saw you first
I did not know what I was looking at
This beauty given to me
Was for your own sake
That I drunken devoured because it seemed
Impossibly good
You hurt me in your expansiveness
In ways I did not know I still ache

I called from the flagstones at midnight
To you upon wrought-iron balconies
You were handing down bread to a begging crowd
I saw you first among its facelessness

In candlelit courtyards
Shaped of many different houses
We are face to face beneath boughs of wisteria
Elegant with restraint
Hand me over these fragile suns

Reach to me
A surge of life
In melodies made of fluent strangers
Mouths full of mystic palettes
Haunting alleyways and reused temples
Holding back a broad and coursing river

Take me by the hand
We might stay like this
The architecture of your miracle
You make of my failures something more
Than you showed me at first.

## Bath

Gulls cry hilarious murder
At the darkened past
With our lights turned off
They sweep the midnight sky

Looking for what food is left of the day

We come back to the same places
Temples on temples
Wishing to keep
What I wish I knew
And you

I dropped a morsel among the cobbles
Eating too fast from hunger
They will scavenge what I lost and laugh.

# Water

# Rehoboth

Old knotted planks lie down
To be overrun with color
Spilled with golden sun
The laughter of an unknown
Child swirls in tide over my persisting shadow

It is the shadow of a gull
Flying low to the cold water
A diver for the secrets
Of dark and pearl shells alike
With the opal of the past

With surpassing mornings
We walk the halls of once and future homes
A band of shells at the surf
That overnumber the hunters
Ornate and tumbling places where life shelters
Places we did not expect to find in ourselves

The wisdom of the waves turns these to sand
Where we built whatever we might lose.

## Mackinac

At midnight
The bowl of sky overturns
Spangled with other futures
You must have
Watched like me long ago
We may find
Shores shine alike brightly
Spilling to earth to the whispering lake
The whole heart of distance
Blowing gently down the long verge
Of the unexplored
Uncurled strands rippling with fresh water
Your upturned face
An island desired

# Clearwater

I lie down for you
The coast
The current of time flows in and out of my side

A certain harbor
The golden sun makes a glow of your distance
Around my wait

Arrive before night
The coast is always young
But the waves will break upon it.

## Michigan

From placid height
I stretch out your curves
To the end of the eye
Infinite hues of white and gray
Black and blue

You cannot be captured
Or confined
I am speechless
And you are the silence of lifetimes

No tracks remain of the days
And nights I crossed your skin
Upon your crests
And in your belly

The frightful power of your life
Covering my face
As I peer forward
Against your evercoming breath
A relentless throb that pulls me
Drenched and sleepless

From a height
My skin is dry
You are not in my eyes my mouth
You untouched.

# South Padre

You were here when I said
I love you and did not know you
Or our weakness
Before you forgave me

The years passed
Because you laid yourself at my mercy
Did it look the same to you then

Across vast and prickly scrublands
Into the lapping gulf
At the end of roads salt dunes and brush
Wandering in a naked wilderness
I cannot find though I am lost in it

A landscape of mysteries I envied in you
Where you went without me because
I could not follow

I came to this faraway place
To know you by your absence
To glimpse the shores of your unknowns
To lie upon them at last.

# Newport

I made a life
Before returning to the coasts
That play with the child
I left and have become
That lay before me in warm sand
Alluring wounds of past and promise

I wade into the ocean
Waves surge around my legs
Tides against the rocks
Carry them away
Caressing with zeal and tenderness

An altered face
In the ocean of sky
Returning to you
Clouds wash like surf
Against the mountains
And your face of heaven.

# Erie

### I

I reached after you
With the arms of a storm
Your arms
Churning the lake to clouds

I followed where the sun sank
Below the waters
To find your death
That the storm did not wish me to find

So the land itself reached out
To close the distance between us

Wrapped in sand and pine
The barren surface
Where I floated helpless
Upon a living sea to crush me in its wake

It made a bay I could not find
A peace I could not make
In your embrace


### II

I sink my vessel
In the harbor you have made
To go beneath your waters

From the misery of cold
And vulnerable

The vessel descends to unapproachable silence
Safe on ribs of sand
In shifting light sparkling through the waves

I hold my breath
As day turns night to day
And after I am gone
The boat rises from the waters.

# Nantucket

You give your gift to me on rooftops
An aria of fire and light
In autumn darkness
Soft candle of your sonorous throat
The wick of your mouth
Glow blanketing brick alleyways
And blind revelries

You give your gift to me
A single small red flower
In the hands of the daughter of songs
A whole creation
That is just for you
To pick just for me
You know no more
Than this perfection of your known world
Than to give it to the one you love

You give your gift to me above seascapes
An island within a horizon of water
We stand upon voyages
Full of the danger of more
A wind bears us up lays low the dunes
To see the boundaries where we sleep and walk
Situated within an endlessness

Your free gift in my upturned hands
Wind playing with your hair
Pulled in strands
A blossom
Heavier than the windhewn stone of wisdom

All that is impossible flies over the rooftops
Out to the unsounded blue of eyes

You give your gift unspoken words
On ecstatic heights where I hear
What you ceaselessly tell me
My life
Consumed by your unconsuming fire
Whose mystery made me
Leave my well for your perilous heights
Where you are
The only water for the thirst you send

You fit unconditional majesty
In my firm and fragile embrace
As a father sees himself
For the first time in a child
After seeing the ends of the earth
I know no more
Than to love the one I know.

# Bodensee

I drank a cup
Made from the hollows of mountains
Filled with tidal rivers
And patience

I dropped the cup in the river I drank
With ages of stone bronze and iron
Currents broke it to pieces

I search the rocky banks
When the tide is out
Find the broken shard of clay
That by its shape suggests
The whole it was

I keep it to marvel
At the mystery of its age
The tides of turbulent rivers
The way it holds all pasts
In its brokenness.

# Laguna

You left something from the ancient
Depth of you upon my shores
This little bit of secret
That you tell
Wispy and intricate
Dashed against the rocks
All you loved in my hard hands

I abandoned something ancient
Of myself
When I swam out far
Before I could remember
A secret told by one who loved me
Not to fear
Either secrets or hardness

We play like children
Where the tide loves the shore
The joy of depths we forgot
Like those who loved us
And their fears.

# Berkeley Springs

You are me
And you are not
Submerged in me
You are not me
And you fill the womb of myself
Holding breath where I emerge

From unknown depths of dark earth
Ethereal steam in frosty night
You blanket me in
The elusive expanse I am
Lying on cold ground spectral stars
Claiming for yourself all futures

A womb that might bear you
A sealed spring that might wash me
Full of something deeply us
Overfull with us
Empty of us.

## Port Washington

You are in my lost places
Beneath a lighthouse
And a harvest moon
Any sign of how we make our way
Toward each other

You are between
The rocks of shores
Others have tried and failed
A path
Hidden in the finding of each other
Battered by tides

I hold but may not possess
Your impossible beauty
A beacon
And a harbor
Could I ever return in the day
The place may be so small
So coarse
If ever I could find it

But once you stretched out
The expanse of my sanctuary
Tender and soft as sugar sand
Among caverns of tearing shore
A pregnant moon
Vast as the waters
A lost place I may forever touch
A place I may not touch
But believe.

# Niagara

Will there always be another time
A morning plays
Golden upon your shoulders
Holding the edges of your face
In crowds and streets
Gardens and ledges
Familiar and new
To see for the first time again
What is ancient and young within myself
Lodged in my own childhood

Is this the last time
I move upward in falling
Persisting in change
Carving a name with the channels of rivers
A path in veils and rainbows
After the flood
The first new day
Feels like it should last
The way of the clear blue I cannot hold
To see you again for the first time.

# Arrivals

# Gratoit

Tumbled upon the raw wideness of nature
Ferns and forest shadows shiver

Horizons bring their promises no nearer
Afraid of the nakedness of newborn sunlight
Sightlines of immortals

Halfway between beginning and end
Journey and destiny a paradise
Indelibly ourselves

In mystery before the world changes
We arrive at one another
Submit to wilderness

We depart on highways unwinding the hidden land
To touch the untouched
To not know

There are places we cannot go back to.

# Nice

All that I might have
If I had not loved you
Is in you
And your eyes I study at midnight

I leave all for you to finish
In my death
When at last I believe in you
Formed from me

In all the time
I might have made myself

All that I have
Has come from how you hide
In my self
And in my searching midnights

And when you leave
You carry what I carried
Into the ends within us
That we have made.

# Edgeworth

Birds take flight with
The afternoon
Swift as your steps
Aimless as early summer

Chased across
Petal-laden greens
They will not be
Caught

Until at last one
That is not afraid
Bluish black limp evening in verdure
And I caught your little hand.

## Myrtle Beach

I walk with you in hunger
Among abundance I may not have

My lips to yours is enough
That fills me
That eats me
So my belly is full and I am empty

Surrounded by you
I am the harbor
That wishes to swallow the sea
So you should not come in

I without
Changing what I am
Must hold of you what I can

The sea does not need the harbor
Like wave after wave you divide
Me again and again
A word upon every tongue
There is always hunger
And there is plenty

And we two meet
Night storms buffet the coast
I burn in bed
In my own abandon
You fed me from nothing
In the morning

The silver horizon drapes
A clear span of distance

Beneath a charcoal sky
You sweep away the abundance
That would destroy me
And there you are
At last alone
My one.

# Moraine

You taught me to cross
From me over to you
To lift us
With the strength of my back
Upon mirrored afternoons
When everything was future

We set out on a wave of sunlight
Toward the love of fathers
And the far landing
Where you cannot go
After you become yourself

A silent cove in the arms of the lake
You held my head in your hands
Where the dark forest met the waters
And burdened clouds
Came over the hills
And rained
So treetops touched the earth

Our boat
A brief solace
Flew upon the water as we rowed
And found festivals in a twisted wreck
Of metal braces and striped fabric
Like standing at a grave
Not knowing what to say
Except what I have been told

The reserve between
Earth and sky
Carrying what has come down to us
Inherited
We went home again in sunlight.

## Emlenton

You were a story
To me in flesh and water
And loss until
I may have seen the place
They told me about

A ruin above stone beaches
Where they used to swim
A place in the sun
Full of weeds

The river valley echoes
Skin pristinely smooth
And the boulders
For jumping

Mirrored water
Slips faster than I am deceived
It pulls me the way you would have

This could be the place
No one could tell
Red leaves falling bloodless toward me
In the river.

# Gettysburg

I bring many ways to you
Lives that might have been
Memories and my own way
That I have

Lost
I stood in your pristine
And scorching fields
The unflinching ardor of youth
The certainty of one
Who expects to die

The lives that stand beside me
Climb into my arms
To be carried
Above the pasts and firsts
Thick as tall grass about my hips

A network of shadows
Made of light
And living and dead
Apart but not alone
The same path

But the face
Passes in and out of changes
And I

Cover the same ground
In surges
Of flesh and despair
Until I am under the waves
Of years that make a life

Until my own face
So much younger
Is new life
Crawling running skipping
Across the distance
At last to return with you.

# Detroit

Days are gone beyond hands
I carry what I left behind
Must leave behind what I have
I look at you to see

How I looked at you when I was young
Like I return to places that have forgotten me
Lights upon the lake
That keep the day in night
That in the night can shine
That do not flee on diffusing waves

How do you weigh me
Against the light and the hurt I gave
From my raw hands
Reaching outward to eternity

What do I possess
But this life I give away

The same unbounded life given me
Another of the generations of hurt and hope
And light divided but undimmed
That cannot stay in your hands
To measure.

## San Juan

A storm swept over
The inside and outside of
Ancient walls at once
There was no place to hide

A crowd gathered within
One of the gates
With the rain like a wall
To the city and to the sea
A stone arch above

Wind and rivulets
Ran through the open doors
Marked on their broad planks
With the date they were made

You swept over me
Leaving no place to hide
My own stony limits were not high
And their reasons meaningless

I met you in the door I left open
You were already inside
You said everything
Will be taken from you
And once
Follow me through the door

I met you under the arch
In a tumult of languages
And faces dripping wet

And I asked
Where are you from
And you asked
Where are you going.